PARACORD CRAFT FACTORY

Everyone loves brightly coloured bracelets to swap with their friends. This booklet is full of lots of inspiration for you to make loads of different things from bracelets to a dog collar. So get creating and enjoy paracord jewellery as it's super easy to do.

Contents

First published 2015 by Guild of Master Craftsman Publications Ltd, Castle Place, 166 High Street, Lewes, East Sussex, BN7 1XU. Copyright in the Work © GMC Publications Ltd, 2015. ISBN 978-1-86108-923-6. All rights reserved. No part of this publication may be reproduced, stored in a retrieval system or transmitted in any form or by any means without the prior permission of the publisher and copyright owner. This book is sold subject to the condition that all designs are copyright and are not for commercial reproduction without the permission of the designer and copyright owner. Whilst every effort has been made to obtain permission from the copyright holders for all material used in this book, the publishers will be pleased to hear from anyone who has not been appropriately acknowledged and to make the correction in future reprints. The publishers and author can accept no legal responsibility for any consequences arising from the application of information, advice or instructions given in this publication. A catalogue record for this book is available from the British Library. Printed in Turkey.

STEP 1
Using 2.4m of 4mm pink/blue cord, open the buckle and thread the cord through the slot on the buckle and back through to make a loop in the cord. Pull the cord until both ends of the cord are level and push the buckle up so there is a small loop of cord on one side.

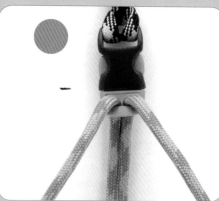

STEP 5
To start braiding, place the cords so one is on the left-hand side and one on the right-hand side of the two centre cords.

COBRA
BRACELET

DIFFICULTY

MAKE A REALLY SIMPLE BRAID
USING A SQUARE KNOT.
BY SIAN HAMILTON

MATERIALS

- 2.4m x 4mm pink/blue paracord
- 15mm x 30mm side-release buckle (in matching colour)
- Small scissors (curved nail scissors)
- Superglue
- Braiding board

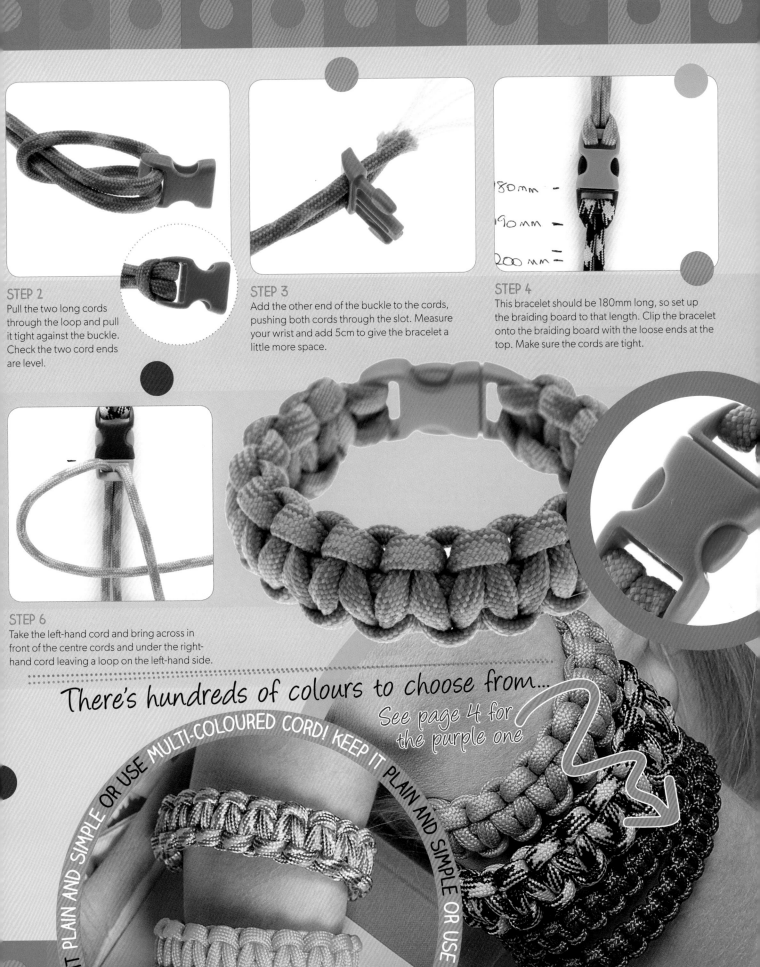

STEP 2
Pull the two long cords through the loop and pull it tight against the buckle. Check the two cord ends are level.

STEP 3
Add the other end of the buckle to the cords, pushing both cords through the slot. Measure your wrist and add 5cm to give the bracelet a little more space.

STEP 4
This bracelet should be 180mm long, so set up the braiding board to that length. Clip the bracelet onto the braiding board with the loose ends at the top. Make sure the cords are tight.

180mm —
190mm —
200 mm —

STEP 6
Take the left-hand cord and bring across in front of the centre cords and under the right-hand cord leaving a loop on the left-hand side.

There's hundreds of colours to choose from...
See page 4 for the purple one

KEEP IT PLAIN AND SIMPLE OR USE MULTI-COLOURED CORD! KEEP IT PLAIN AND SIMPLE OR USE MULTI

STEP 7

Bring the right-hand cord across behind the centre cords and through the loop in the left-hand cord. Pull tight.

STEP 8

Take the right-hand cord and bring across in front of the centre cords and under the left-hand cord leaving a loop on the right-hand side.

STEP 9

Bring the left-hand cord across behind the centre cords and through the loop in the right-hand cord. Pull tight.

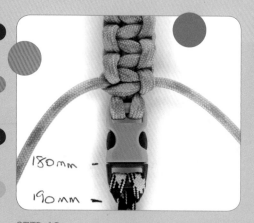

180mm —

190mm —

STEP 10

Repeat Steps 6 to 9 until you have reached the end (up to the bottom buckle). You will need to pull hard on the left and right-hand cords to make the knots tight.

STEP 11

Unclip the bracelet from the braiding board. Give a good hard tug on both the side cords and cut off as close to the braid as possible.

Extra project

To make a double bracelet, use a thinner 2mm cord and follow the main project but make two braids side by side on one buckle.

STEP 12

Finally put a little drop of superglue on the cut ends to stop them coming apart when you wear the bracelet.

THE PURPLE ONE! - EXTRA PROJECT

EXTRA PROJECT -

MIX & MATCH COLOURS TO MAKE THE BRACELET YOU WANT! MIX & MATCH COLOURS TO

TRY DIFFERENT COLOURS AND STYLES TO MAKE COOL BRACELETS

MATERIALS
- 3m x 4mm yellow paracord
- 1.5m x 2mm red paracord
- 20mm side-release buckle
- Small scissors (curved nail scissors)
- Superglue
- Braiding board

DIFFICULTY

★ ★ ★ ★

SIDE KNOT BRACELET

CREATE A WIDE BAND BRACELET

WITH TWO COLOURS OF CORD.

BY SIAN HAMILTON

YOUR MAIN PROJECT - TURN OVER TO SEE HOW TO MAKE!

DID YOU KNOW?

THE KNOT USED IN THIS BRACELET IS CALLED A REVERSED HALF-HITCH KNOT.

See page 7 for your CHUNKY BRACELET

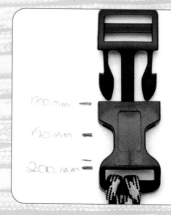

STEP 1

Open the buckle and take the piece that has a flat end. Thread a piece of spare paracord through from the side, then clip this cord to the edge of your braiding board.

STEP 2

Cut two pieces of 4mm yellow paracord and one piece of 2mm red paracord 1.5m long. Fold each cord in half and push the fold through the loop in the buckle from the back. Pull the cord ends through the loop and pull tight. Do the two yellow ones first then the red one in the middle. It may be a bit of a squeeze.

STEP 3

Take the other piece of the buckle (the part that looks like a fork) and using another spare buckle and piece of cord, attach it to the other end of your braiding board. Clip it at the right length for the bracelet you want to make. Make the bracelet about 5cm bigger than your wrist.

STEP 7

With the bottom secure, go back to the top to start the knotting. Take the left outside cord and bring in front of the left centre cord, around the back and through the loop created in the left cord. Pull tight.

STEP 8

Using the same left outside cord, bring it behind the left centre cord, through the middle and back in front of the left centre cord. Take it through the loop and pull tight. This is the knot you will be making for the whole bracelet.

STEP 9

Repeat Steps 7 and 8 to create an identical knot on the right centre cord.

STEP 13

Keep repeating the same knotting order, left yellow cord, right yellow cord, left red cord then right red cord. As you repeat the red knots swap the cords over to make a cross going down the middle.

STEP 14

When you have reached the end, make sure the last knot is a yellow one. The yellow cords should be facing outward from the sides. The red cords in the middle need to be pushed through to the back.

STEP 15

Tie the red cords together and add glue to hold them in place. Add glue to all four pieces of yellow cord where the cord comes out of the knot. When the glue is dry, cut the cords off as close to the knotting as you can.

STEP 4
Thread the two inside yellow cords through the bottom loop (rectangular shaped hole), on the buckle from the back; these are the centre cords.

STEP 5
Bring the yellow centre cords back up through the top loop from the front to the back. If your buckle only has one loop then bring the cords through the loop from the back and move straight to Step 6.

STEP 6
Take the left-hand cord and bring the end around the back of the left centre cord, across in front of the cord and take the end behind the loop created by the cord and pull tight. Repeat for the right-hand cord.

STEP 10
If you remember that each knot goes over the centre cord and around the back for the first part of the knot, and under the centre cord and around the front for the second part, it'll be easier to do.

STEP 11
After doing a knot on each side with the yellow cords, you now need to do the same with the red cords, knotting them around the centre yellow cords. Take the left red cord and follow Steps 7 and 8.

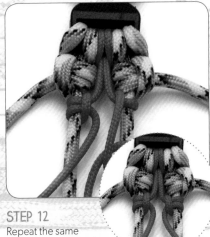

STEP 12
Repeat the same process to make a knot using the right red cord around the right yellow centre cord. Pull each knot tight before making the next knot.

STYLE VARIATION 2
To make this bracelet into a chunkier style, use 4mm cords and a bigger buckle.

To make a smaller bracelet use all 2mm cords, making the outside colour different to the middle colour and use a 15mm buckle.

STYLE VARIATION 1

TOP TIP! SEAL BOTH ENDS OF EACH CORD WITH GLUE BEFORE YOU START, TO STOP THEM FRAYING.

WHY NOT MAKE THESE STYLES FOR YOUR PET?

Fishtail
BRACELET

MAKE A TWO-COLOUR FISHTAIL DESIGN.

BY SIAN HAMILTON

MATERIALS
- 1.5m x 3mm blue and green paracord
- 15mm side-release buckle in the same colour
- Bulldog clip
- Tape measure
- Blunt-ended scissors
- Superglue

DIFFICULTY
★ ★ ★

TOP TIP!
Glue ends before you start to stop the cord from fraying.

STEP 1
Take the green and blue paracord and glue the ends together, pressing them flat as the glue dries. You can use the side of the scissors and press against something hard (such as a plate) to get the ends flat. Let the glue dry then put one flat end over the other and use more glue to stick them together. It's best to do this in two stages to stop them coming apart. Use the scissors to trim the sides when the glue has dried so the cord is the same width all the way along.

STEP 2
Fold the cord in half just to the side of the glued section and push through one piece of the buckle. Pull the two cord ends through the loop and pull tight.

STEP 3
Take the other end of the buckle and pull the cords through from the back so they are coming towards you. Pull them through until the cords between both buckle pieces measure your wrist size, plus 5cm.

For the girls... Change the colours to match your favourite outfit or make for a best friend

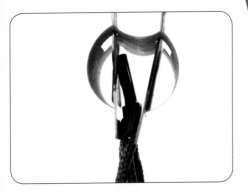

STEP 4
Place the buckle end with the loose cords in the bulldog clip. You want the clip to hold onto both the buckle and the cords so they don't slip around. Check the measurement of the cords between the buckle pieces is the correct size.

STEP 5
Take the two loose cords (weaving cords) through the middle of the cords attached to the buckle (centre cords) and bring the green cord to the left-hand side and the blue cord to the right. The blue cord needs to be behind the green cord.

STEP 6
Bring the green weaving cord on the left-hand side over the centre blue cord and under the centre green cord. When it's on the right, it should be sitting below the blue weaving cord.

STEP 7
Pull the green weaving cord and wiggle it up tight to the bulldog clip. Bring the blue weaving cord on the right-hand side over the green centre cord and under the blue centre cord. Go back under the green centre cord. Pull tight and push up at far as it will go. The braid will hold in place after a few weaves.

STEP 8
From this point onwards, remember that the weaving cords always finish on the right-hand side. Next take the green weaving cord, go over the centre green, under the centre blue, back over the centre blue and under the centre green.

STEP 9
Repeat Steps 7 and 8 with the weaving cords, using the blue next, then the green, then the blue and carry on until you have filled the bracelet and reached the buckle. As you get close to the end, use blunt-ended scissors to help poke the cords through the middle of the braid, as the gap gets tighter. Keep going until you really can't get any more cords through the middle. Finish with the weaving cords at the back of the bracelet and glue to stop them coming undone, then cut off any excess cord.

INFINITY BRACELET

MAKE AN INFINITY BRACELET TO SHARE AND SWAP WITH YOUR FRIENDS.

BY SIAN HAMILTON

KEEP IT SIMPLE AND USE ONE COLOUR OR MIX IT UP BY USING TWO COLOURS OR MULTI-COLOURED CORD!

MAKE FOR BOYS & GIRLS · HUNDREDS OF COLOURS TO CHOOSE FROM!

MATERIALS

- 24cm x 4mm green paracord
- 22cm x 4mm pink/blue paracord
- 2 x small matching colour side-release buckles
- C-lon beading thread (or sewing thread) in matching colours
- Small scissors (curved nail scissors)
- Superglue

DIFFICULTY

★

STEP 1

Cut a piece of 4mm green paracord 24cm long and seal both ends with superglue so the white inner cords are not showing.

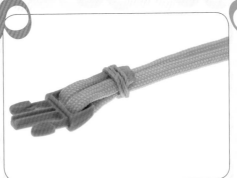

STEP 2

Push both cord ends through one side of a buckle (with the end that looks like a fork). Get a small rubber band (ones used for loom band bracelets are good) and wrap around the ends to hold them in place.

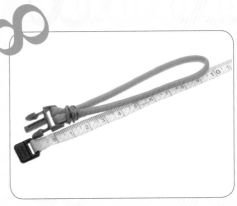

STEP 3

Make sure the cord loop measures 10cm from the bit where the cords go through the buckle to the end of the cord loop. This will make the finished bracelet 18cm long; you can make it longer or shorter to fit your wrist.

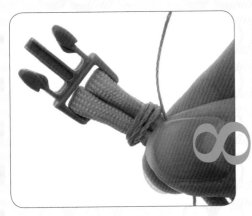

STEP 4

Take a 20cm piece of beading thread and hold it against the cords with your thumb and fingers.

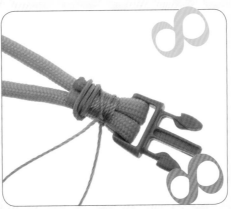

STEP 5

Wrap the thread around the cords between the rubber band and buckle as tightly as you can. Knot the two ends of thread together.

STEP 6

Place a tiny bit of superglue on the knot and cut off the ends of thread.

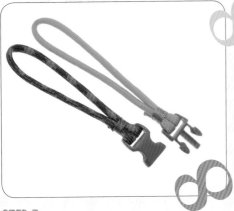

STEP 7

Make a second piece the same way using the pink/blue cord and blue buckle end. This one needs to measure 10cm from the end of the buckle to the cord loop.

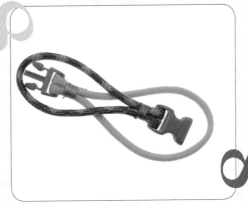

STEP 8

To make them into a bracelet, place them on a table with both buckle ends sitting inside the cord loops.

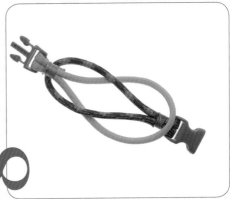

STEP 9

Take hold of both buckles through the loops and pull tight.

Why not? Make the cord longer to make a necklace!

Simply double up the cords to make a thicker bracelet. It's more tricky to get four cords through the end of the small buckle. You can buy a bigger buckle if you really can't get the cords to fit through the small one.

TOP TIP!

Try some different colour combinations for a completely different look.

PHOTOGRAPHS: ROSIE WOOLDRIDGE, SIAN HAMILTON

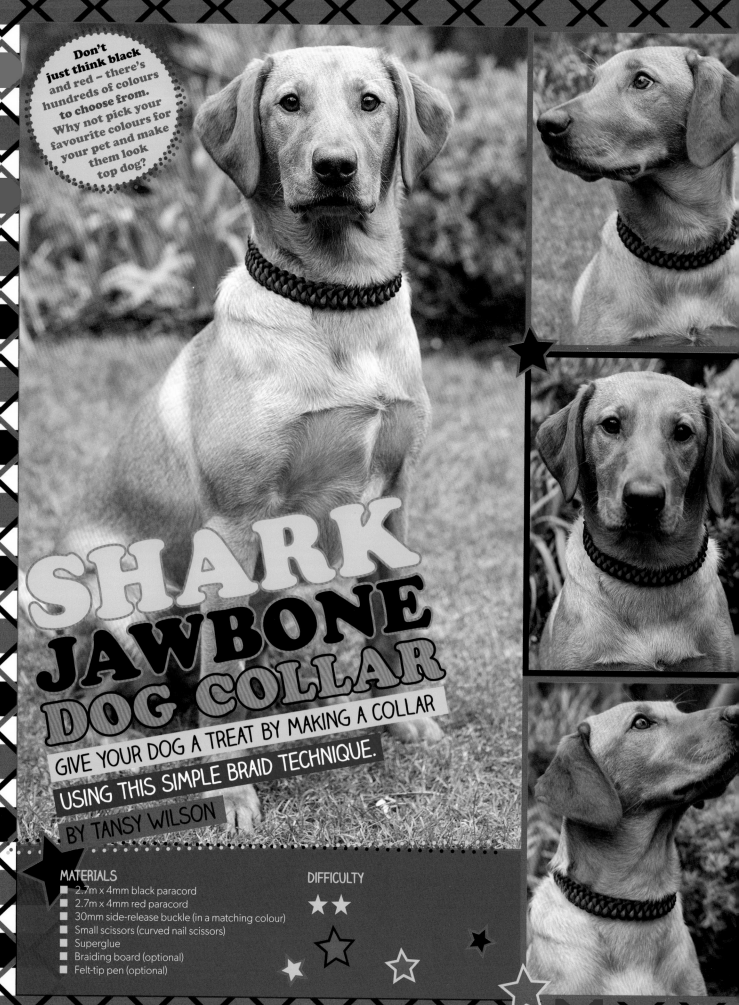

Don't just think black and red – there's hundreds of colours to choose from. Why not pick your favourite colours for your pet and make them look top dog?

SHARK JAWBONE DOG COLLAR

GIVE YOUR DOG A TREAT BY MAKING A COLLAR USING THIS SIMPLE BRAID TECHNIQUE.

BY TANSY WILSON

MATERIALS

- 2.7m x 4mm black paracord
- 2.7m x 4mm red paracord
- 30mm side-release buckle (in a matching colour)
- Small scissors (curved nail scissors)
- Superglue
- Braiding board (optional)
- Felt-tip pen (optional)

DIFFICULTY

★★

STEP 1
Take one of the 2.7m lengths of 4mm red paracord and and pull out 5cm of the inner white strands from one end of the cord and cut them off. Slide the red casing back into position leaving an empty tube.

STEP 2
Add superglue to one end of black cord so when it is dry it becomes rigid. Insert this rigid end into the empty tube space created in Step 1. Glue together and leave to dry.

STEP 3
When completely dry, hold the cord near to the join and form a loop. Hold one half of the buckle so the right side is facing up and push the loop down and away from you through the buckle.

STEP 4
Pass both ends of the cord through the loop and pull all the way through, pulling tightly so the join is now just hidden under the loop created in Step 3.

STEP 5
Hold the other half of the buckle again so the right side is facing up and pass the two cord ends down through the buckle.

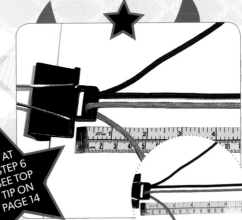

AT STEP 6 SEE TOP TIP ON PAGE 14

STEP 6
Pull the ends through until you are left with two straight, parallel, untwisted cords both approx. 40cm in length. You may find it easier to do this by clipping the buckle ends onto a braiding board that is the same length as your finished collar will be.

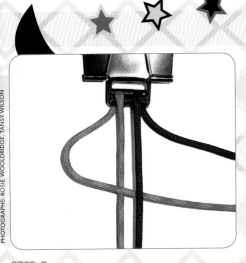

STEP 7
Now you are ready to start weaving. Whatever colour you want to be on the inside of the weave design is the cord you need to start with. We will start with the red cord. Take this cord and pass it over itself (the straight cord between the buckles) and then under the other straight (black) cord.

STEP 8
Now take the black cord and pass it over the red cord that has just been used coming out of the weave. Keep it on top of the straight black cord and then pass it under the straight red cord and out the other side.

STEP 9
Still holding this black cord, thread it up through the red loop formed in Step 7.

PHOTOGRAPHS: ROSIE WOOLDRIDGE, TANSY WILSON

STEP 10

Pull both cord ends together so the knot tightens onto the two straight cords between the buckles. Use your fingers to slide the knot up to rest snugly under the buckle.

STEP 11

Repeat Steps 6 to 9, always ensuring you start each woven knot with the red cord until you reach the other end. As you get close to the other end it may be easier to unclip the collar from the board.

STEP 12

Push the cords for the final knot through so they come out at the back of the collar. Give them both a hard tug and cut them off as close to the braid as possible. You can use a felt-tip pen to colour the white inner strands if they show. Finally put a little drop of superglue on the cut ends to stop them coming apart.

Change your size!
TOP TIP!

The length of cord used makes a collar of 45cm, which will fit a medium-sized dog. At Step 6 check to see if the collar fits your dog's neck and make it longer or shorter before clipping to the board.

Why not?
Make bracelets too...

You will need **4m of each colour cord to make an 18cm bracelet.**

WHY NOT MAKE A BRACELET? DON'T FORGET ALL THE COLOUR COMBINATIONS YOU CAN COME UP WITH!

14

Your step-by-steps are on pages 16-17 for this colourway but just see how many colours you can choose from

HUNDREDS OF COLOUR COMBINATIONS TO CHOOSE FROM!

DASH OF COLOUR BRACELET

USE TWO COLOURS OF CORD TO MAKE A COBRA-STYLE BRACELET WITH A DASHED LINE IN A DIFFERENT COLOUR.

BY SIAN HAMILTON

MATERIALS

- 42cm x 4mm yellow paracord
- 1.5m x 4mm pink/turquoise paracord
- 15mm side-release buckle (in matching colour)
- Small scissors (curved nail scissors)
- Superglue
- Braiding board

DIFFICULTY

★

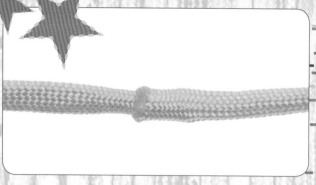

STEP 1

To make the inner cord (dash colour), take the 4mm yellow parcord and cut to 42cm long. Push one end of cord inside the other so the cord is a big loop, and glue in place.

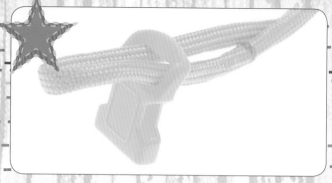

STEP 2

Flatten the cord into a line with the join in the centre and pull one end through one piece of the buckle.

STEP 5

Repeat Steps 2 to 4 for the other end of the cord and the other piece of buckle. You should now have a bracelet made of a double cord.

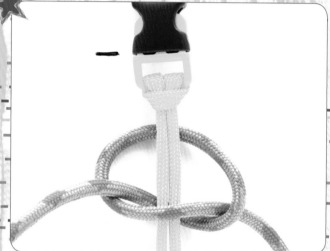

STEP 6

Attach the bracelet to the braiding board. Take the pink/turquoise cord and fold in half. Hold the cord at the halfway point and place that point behind the yellow cord on the board. Take the left-hand pink/turquoise cord over the yellow and bring the right-hand pink/turquoise cord in front of the left-hand cord and behind the yellow. Take through the loop made by the left-hand pink/turquoise cord. Pull tight.

STEP 9

On the first part of the knot, remember that when the left cord goes across the front that you don't push it through the yellow cords. Only do this when the right-hand cord comes across the front.

STEP 10

Keep going with these knots to the end. Try to finish on a knot with the pink/turquoise cord in front of the yellow cord, as it looks neater.

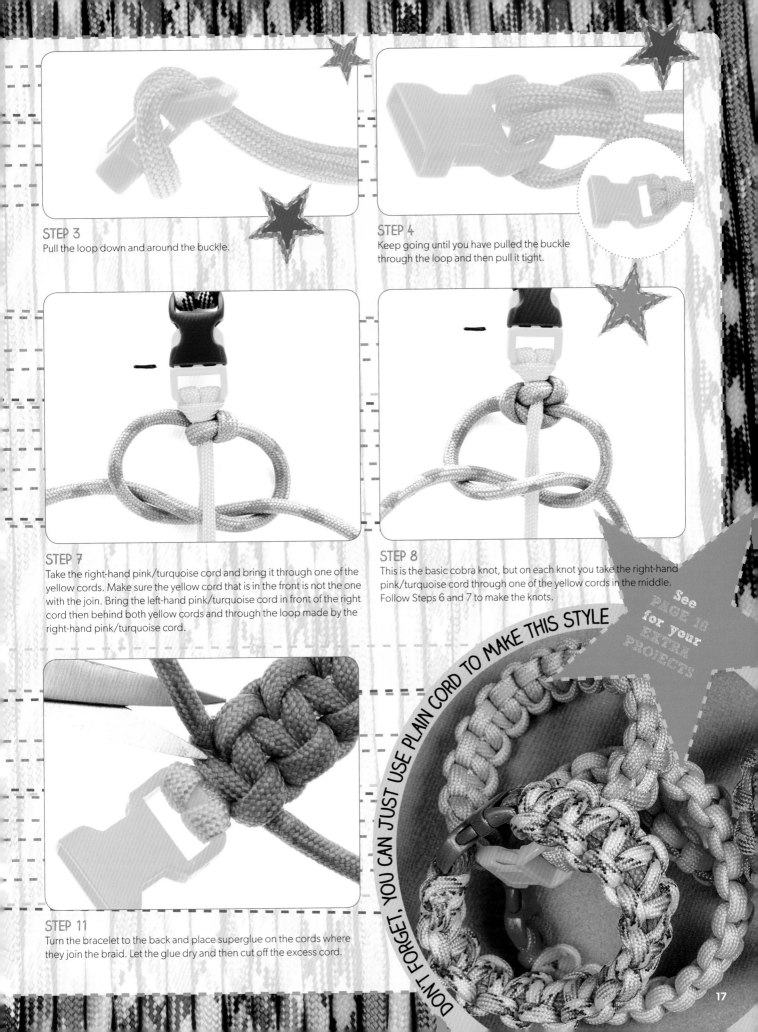

STEP 3

Pull the loop down and around the buckle.

STEP 4

Keep going until you have pulled the buckle through the loop and then pull it tight.

STEP 7

Take the right-hand pink/turquoise cord and bring it through one of the yellow cords. Make sure the yellow cord that is in the front is not the one with the join. Bring the left-hand pink/turquoise cord in front of the right cord then behind both yellow cords and through the loop made by the right-hand pink/turquoise cord.

STEP 8

This is the basic cobra knot, but on each knot you take the right-hand pink/turquoise cord through one of the yellow cords in the middle. Follow Steps 6 and 7 to make the knots.

STEP 11

Turn the bracelet to the back and place superglue on the cords where they join the braid. Let the glue dry and then cut off the excess cord.

DON'T FORGET, YOU CAN JUST USE PLAIN CORD TO MAKE THIS STYLE

See PAGE 18 for your EXTRA PROJECTS

17

Why not...
make a belt the same way

Just make the middle (yellow) cords about 10cm longer than your waist. When braiding, take the side cords through one middle cord each time. So, in Step 8 when it says take the left-hand pink/turquoise across the front to the right, take it through one of the middle cords instead. Then on the next knot take the right-hand cord you used in the previous knot). On this belt you use both middle cords one after the other. This makes the nice double-dash pattern.

MAKE A CHANGE - USE THIS PROJECT TO MAKE THE NORMAL COBRA BRACELET ON PAGE 2

Vary it...

You can use this pattern to make a normal cobra bracelet. Don't take the side cords through a middle cord but always bring them across the front as you would with a normal single colour cobra bracelet (as on page 2).

DRAGONFLY CLIPS

MAKE THESE CLEVER DRAGONFLIES BY ADAPTING THE SIMPLE COBRA KNOT TECHNIQUE. BY TANSY WILSON

MATERIALS
- 1m x 3mm pink paracord
- 2 x large hole blue beads
- Hairclip
- Cotton thread and dressmaker's needle
- Small scissors (curved nail scissors)
- Superglue

DIFFICULTY ★

See page 21 for how to make the larger dragonfly

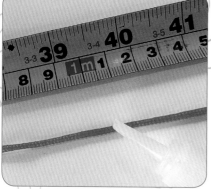

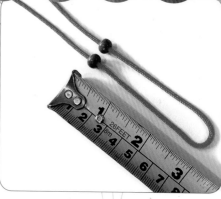

STEP 1

Take the length of 3mm pink paracord and add a drop of superglue at the 1m mark and leave to dry. This means that once it is dry, you can cut the cord and it won't fray. Add a drop of superglue at the other end too. Cut cord to 1m.

STEP 2

Thread two matching beads onto the 1m cord and fold the cord in half so the beads sit at the fold.

STEP 3

Move each bead up and away from the centre fold approx. 8cm, so there is a bead on each cord length.

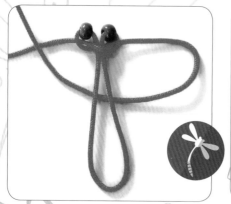

STEP 7

Now start with the right-hand cord and pass it under the long loop and over the left-hand cord.

STEP 8

Then take the left-hand cord and pass it over the long loop and under the right-hand cord.

STEP 9

Pull both cord ends together so the knot tightens onto the long loop. Use your fingers to slide the knot up to rest snugly under the knot under the beads.

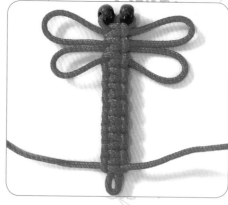

STEP 13

Slide this tightened knot up the long loop to meet the first knot made.

STEP 14

Repeat Steps 10 to 13 to create another set of wings. Again, make sure you slide the knots up the long loop so they sit tight together.

STEP 15

Repeat Steps 4 to 6 to continue knotting all the way down the long loop to form the body. Give a good hard tug on both cords and cut off as close to the braid as possible and add a drop of superglue to each end to stop them from fraying. Finally glue or sew onto a hairclip using matching cotton.

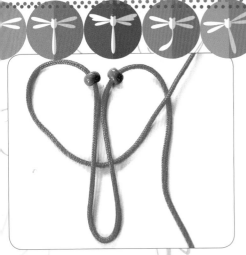

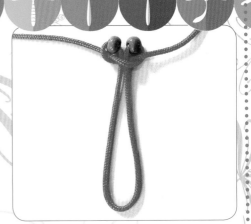

STEP 4

Pinch the two cords directly under the beads creating a long loop and take the left-hand cord and pass it under the long loop and over the right-hand cord.

STEP 5

Take the right-hand cord and pass it over the long loop and under the left-hand cord. This means you are threading the right-hand cord through the loop created in Step 4.

STEP 6

Pull both the ends together so the knot tightens under the beads added in Step 2. You need to make sure the beads stay sitting at the top.

STEP 10

Repeat Steps 4 and 5 so you start with the left-hand cord going under the long loop and over the right-hand cord. Then take the right-hand cord and go over the long loop and under the left-hand cord. Do not pull these cords tight.

STEP 11

Repeat Steps 7 and 8 so you take the right-hand cord and go under the long loop and over the left-hand cord. Then take the left-hand cord and go over the long loop and under the right-hand cord. Again do not pull really tight.

STEP 12

Open the knot up created in Step 10 so you pull it to create a pair of wings. This will also tighten the knot below.

Swap colours

Change the colour of the cord to match your outfit!

Why not?

Use 4mm paracord to make large dragonflies. These can be sewn onto a brooch back to make lovely presents for all your family and friends.

21

BAGS of STYLE

MAKE A SMALL BAG USING FINE CORD WITH A LONG STRAP THAT GOES ACROSS YOUR BODY.

BY SIAN HAMILTON

MATERIALS
- 27m x 2mm white paracord
- 20m x 2mm pink paracord
- 8m x 2mm purple paracord
- 2 x 45mm pink carabiner clips
- Two-hole button
- Superglue
- 1 x 40mm and 1 x 20mm foldback clip
- Small scissors (curved nail scissors)
- Tape measure

DIFFICULTY
★★★★★

DON'T JUST MAKE IT IN THESE COLOURS, THINK OF ALL THE OTHER COMBOS

See page 24 for your BRACELET

STEP 1

Cut 16 pink, 24 white and 8 purple cords, each 1m in length. Using the two pink cords and the foldback clip, fold both cords in half and place side by side in the clip.

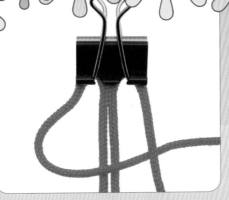

STEP 2

Start a standard cobra knot by taking the left-side cord across in front of the two centre cords and behind the right-side cord.

STEP 3

Bring the right-side cord behind the two centre cords and through the loop made in the left-side cord.

STEP 4

Pull the cords tight and start the second part of the cobra knot. Bring the right-side cord in front of the centre cords and behind the left-side cord.

STEP 5

Bring the left-side cord behind the centre cords and through the loop made in the right-side cord.

STEP 6

Pull tight. This is the cobra knot completed. Take the cords out of the clip and make sure the knot is tight. Pull on the two centre cords to remove the loops left by the clip. Now repeat Steps 1 to 6 for all the cords. You need to make 8 pink sets, 12 white sets and 4 purple sets.

PHOTOGRAPHS: ROSIE WOOLDRIDGE, SIAN HAMILTON

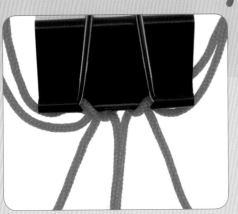

STEP 7

When all the sets are made, take two pink sets and place them in the bigger foldback clip side by side. Find the four centre cords; these will be two from each set (knots that are sitting in the clip).

STEP 8

Check you are using the right cords before continuing. Check Step 9 picture to see what this should look like finished. Now make another cobra knot using Steps 2 to 5.

STEP 9

Pull the knots tight and release from the clip. You should have a piece that looks like this. Now make all the sets from Step 6 in the same way. You need to do 6 pieces in white, 2 pieces in pink and 4 pieces with one purple and one pink set. When finished you should have 12 pieces with three knots that look like this.

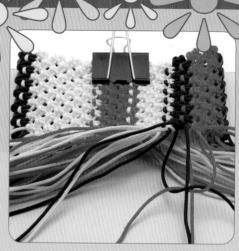

STEP 10

Now you need to start joining all the pieces from Step 9 together. Take a pink piece and a white piece and place in the clip. Find the two ends of the pink cords and white cords that are sitting by each other and make another complete cobra knot with them (follow Steps 2 to 5).

STEP 11

This can get a little complicated so take it slowly. Take the piece from Step 10 with pink on the left and white on the right and add pieces, always to the right side (using Step 10 instructions) in this order: white set, purple/pink set (with purple on the left), purple/pink set (with pink on the left), white set, pink set, white set, white set, purple/pink set (with purple on the left), purple/pink set (with pink on the left), white set. When you get to here, join the two ends together (that should be white on the left and pink on the right) and make a knot to complete the circle.

STEP 12

You now have the beginnings of the bag and should have a complete ring of knotted cords. Now just keep going around in a circle knotting alternate cords, so the pattern becomes a criss-cross. This is easier to do if you clip the whole thing to a board and keep moving the bag around so the part you are working on is at the front. Each row should have row of knots above, between the rows.

STEP 14

Now you need to tie the bottom up. Turn the bag upside down so the cords are facing you and flatten it so the two sides sit together. Find the four very end cords and start knotting using exactly the same knot (cobra) as you have so far. Make a complete cobra knot and each time use the next four cords along the bottom. Make sure you pull all the knots as tight as you can and keep knotting until you reach the end.

STEP 15

To make sure the bottom of the bag doesn't come undone you will need to glue it carefully. Using superglue make sure you glue each cord right at the point where it goes into the knot. Let the glue dry completely.

STEP 16

Take a small pair of scissors and cut off all the cords as close to the knots as you can. Don't worry if they stick out a bit, as this is the inside of the bag.

TOP TIP!
THIS BAG IS APPROX. 11CM HIGH BY 15CM WIDE. TO MAKE IT BIGGER USE LONGER PIECES OF CORD AND ADD MORE SETS AT STEP 6.

Why not?

MAKE A NICE BRACELET USING THE HANDLE BRAID

START AT STEP 19 but fold the cords over a pencil instead of a carabiner clip. Continue to make cobra knots until the braid can wrap around your wrist three times. Take the pencil out of the end and cut the cords flat with a pair of scissors. Cut the other end off flat too and glue both ends into a magnetic barrel clasp that has open ends for cord to sit into. Superglue will work with this style of magnetic clasp.

STEP 13

It can be very easy to knot the wrong cords, so go slowly. If you go wrong just undo the knots one at a time until you reach the one that's wrong and start again. Stop when the bag is as deep as you want it or when you have about 10cm left on the cords.

STEP 17

Now you need to turn the bag inside out. These cords are quite stiff so this will be a little difficult. Push the glued bottom up through the middle and roll the outsides down.

Make your bracelet in whatever colour you like...

STEP 18

Once you have done that, the bag has the glued ends on the inside. Take a pencil and with the blunt end (not the part you write with) push the corners of the bag out a bit by placing the pencil on the inside of the bag and pushing gently until the bottom looks level. The bag part is now finished.

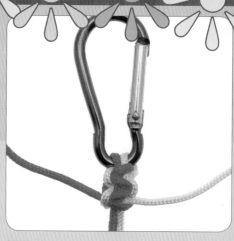

STEP 19

To make the handle, take a carabiner and cut 3m lengths of pink and white cord. Fold both the cords so there is 1m on one side and 2m on the other. Place the carabiner in the fold so the two cords are looped through the carabiner. You want the inside centre cords to be the 1m cords with the 2m cords to be on the outside – they are ones you will knot with. The pink is on the left and the white on the right.

STEP 20

Now use the same cobra knot to make the handle (follow Steps 2 to 5). To begin with it will be hard as the cords are really long! If you have a piece of board available, use the 40mm foldback clip to hold the carabiner to the edge of the board.

STEP 21

When you have about 15cm left on the centre cords, stop. Take the other carabiner and bring the centre cords through it. Start to knot these cords exactly as you did for the other end.

STEP 22

Make about three knots and then go back to the other cords and knot until they meet. Glue the cords where they meet the knots and then cut off the cord ends with a pair of scissors. The carabiner clips will fit nicely through the holes in the bag sides. You could make lots of different length handles for your bag as you can change them easily.

STEP 23

If you want to have a closer for the bag, get a two-hole button and thread a small piece of cord through it so the cord is coming out of the back of the button. Push the cord through the bag in the centre between the handles (you might want to measure this), taking one cord through a hole and the other cord through the hole below.

STEP 24

Knot the cords together on the inside and glue to secure. Cut off the excess thread.

STEP 25

Take a short piece of cord and thread through two holes side by side on the opposite side to where you just put the button. Leave a loop in the cord about 5cm long. With the bag lying flat and the loop in the cord facing you, take the two ends of this same piece of cord and make one cobra knot using the loop as the centre cords. This will hold the loop in place. Glue and cut off the excess cord.

GLOBE KNOT PENDANT

TRY THIS MORE TECHNICAL BRAID TO MAKE A BALL KNOT NECKLACE.

BY TANSY WILSON

MATERIALS

- 1.5m x 4mm blue paracord
- 2 x large holed beads
- Small scissors (curved nail scissors)
- Superglue

DIFFICULTY

★★★☆☆

See page 28 for how to make your GLOBE KNOT PENDANT and add the beads...

HUNDREDS OF COLOURS TO CHOOSE FROM SO GET MIXING AND MATCHING!

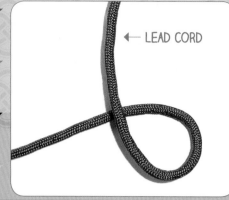

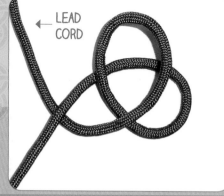

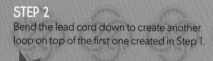

STEP 1

Use 1.5m of blue 4mm paracord and make a small loop at the centrepoint. Hold the cord that's pointing north in this photograph and always use this cord to do the following steps. Call this the lead cord.

STEP 2

Bend the lead cord down to create another loop on top of the first one created in Step 1.

STEP 3

Thread the lead cord underneath the non-used length to form this pattern.

STEP 7

Follow the exact same weave, going over at the top then under and over to come out at the bottom with the lead cord facing left.

STEP 8

Continue round, passing under the unused cord.

STEP 9

Pass the lead cord over the double cords on the left side of the central loop. Then continue going under and over until you get all the way around with the lead cord going under the double cords on the left-hand side.

STEP 11

Pull the cord in their pairs starting from the knot made in Step 10 so you tighten the entire weave.

STEP 12

When the weave is tight with no gaps at all you can push the centre by the knot so it starts to form a dome around the knot.

STEP 13

Work the weave with your fingers so you start to form a ball shape. You may need to pull the cords again to keep the weave tight with no gaps until you achieve a perfect ball.

Top tip! This tricky knot takes quite a lot of patience to complete, so don't worry if you don't get it right first time.

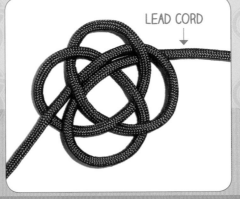

STEP 4

Thread the lead cord down through the central loop. Weave it behind and then over the right side of the central loop, then go underneath the outer loop on the right side to come out the other end.

STEP 5

Hold the lead cord down and take it left and weave it over the left loop and then behind and then over and behind the cords, forming the central loop. Come out top right of the right side loop, creating a fourth loop at the bottom.

STEP 6

With the four loops in place you can weave the lead cord around the initial loops you created in exactly the same way so you will start to form a double line of cords going around.

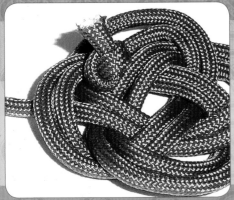

STEP 10

Turn the weave over and tie a knot in the lead cord as close to the weave as possible and then cut away the excess cord.

STEP 14

Thread two pretty beads onto the long end of cord and then, holding it against the ball, make sure it goes over your head. If it is too long you can cut some excess cord away. Add a drop of superglue to the cord end and leave to dry so it goes hard and rigid. Once dry, you can poke it into the ball and superglue into place.

Adding those beads!

You can add as many beads as you like to the long end of cord before gluing into place. You will need an even number of beads on each side of the necklace. Once glued the beads will have a symmetrical pattern on each cord.

ADDING BEADS! VARIATION - ADDING BEADS! VARIATION

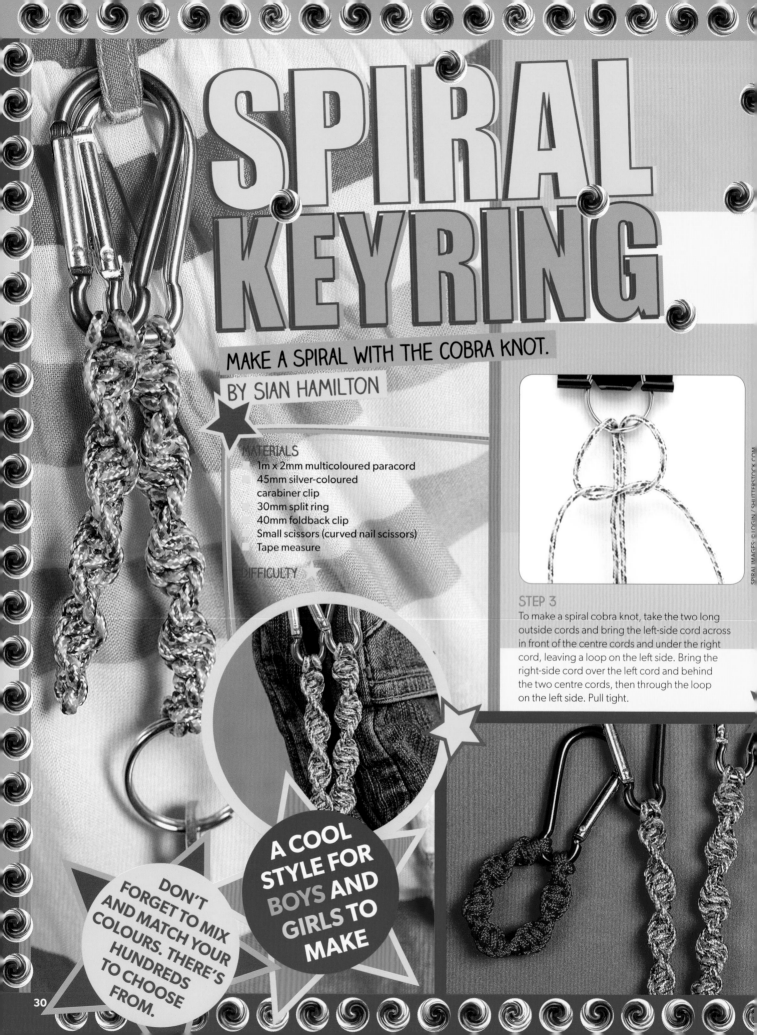

SPIRAL KEYRING

MAKE A SPIRAL WITH THE COBRA KNOT.

BY SIAN HAMILTON

MATERIALS

- 1m x 2mm multicoloured paracord
- 45mm silver-coloured carabiner clip
- 30mm split ring
- 40mm foldback clip
- Small scissors (curved nail scissors)
- Tape measure

DIFFICULTY ★

STEP 3

To make a spiral cobra knot, take the two long outside cords and bring the left-side cord across in front of the centre cords and under the right cord, leaving a loop on the left side. Bring the right-side cord over the left cord and behind the two centre cords, then through the loop on the left side. Pull tight.

A COOL STYLE FOR BOYS AND GIRLS TO MAKE

DON'T FORGET TO MIX AND MATCH YOUR COLOURS. THERE'S HUNDREDS TO CHOOSE FROM.

STEP 1
Take 1m of 2mm cord and fold in half. Take the loop through the carabiner clip and push both cord ends through the loop. Pull tight.

STEP 2
Using a braiding board, clip the split ring to the edge of the board with the foldback clip. Pull both cord ends through the split ring from the back and make the gap between the carabiner clip and the split ring 5cm.

5cm

STEP 4
Repeat Step 3 for the whole length of the braid. As you make more knots the whole braid will start to twist. You must always bring the left-side cord in front of the centre cords and the right-side cord behind the centre.

STEP 5
Keep going until you reach the carabiner clip. Cut off the excess cord and add superglue to the ends to stop the braid coming undone.

SEE PAGE 2 FOR HELP WITH THE BRACELET

Why not?
Make a spiral bracelet using the project on page 2, but keep repeating Steps 6 and 7 to make the braid spiral. Finish the bracelet following Steps 10 to 12.

How about?

MAKE A BAG CHARM, BUT WITHOUT ADDING A SPLIT RING TO THE BRAID.
To make a spiral without a split ring, place a pencil where the split ring should be (in Step 2) and loop the cord over that, making sure the cord is looped over from the back. Hold the pencil in place with the foldback clip and continue with the steps to do about three knots. When you have a few knots done, pull the pencil out and pull on the centre cords while pushing the knots away from the carabiner clip until the loops left at the end (where the pencil was) close up. Continue with the braid following the project instructions.

WHY NOT MAKE A BAG CHARM? WHY NOT MAKE A BAG CHARM? WHY NOT MAKE A BAG CHARM? WHY NOT MAKE

Turk's Head RING

USE THIS CLEVER TECHNIQUE TO CREATE A NEVER-ENDING WAVY PATTERN FOR A RING.

BY TANSY WILSON

MATERIALS

- 1.2m x 4mm red paracord
- Cylinder
- Rubber band
- Craft knife or small scissors (curved nail scissors)
- Superglue

DIFFICULTY

★★★★

Cut 4m of cord and wrap around a larger cylindrical object to make a bangle. A diameter of 7cm will make a bangle for a small wrist. You can keep following the wavy pattern to have three or even four rows of cord like this bangle.

WHY NOT TRY MAKING A MATCHING BRACELET! WHY NOT TRY MAKING A MATCHING BRACELET! WHY NOT TRY MAKING A MATCHING BRACELET! WHY NOT TRY M

STEP 1

Use 1.2m of 4mm red paracord and add superglue to each end to stop the cord from fraying. When the glue is dry, secure one end of the cord to a cylindrical object approx. 2cm in diameter. You can use a rubber band to hold it in place.

STEP 2

Take the long end of cord and wrap it around the back of your cylinder and continue to wrap around to the front, crossing itself at the front.

STEP 3

Continue wrapping this long end back around the cylinder and coming up at the front to form two parallel lines at the front.

STEP 4

Pass the long end under the right-hand diagonal of cord and pull the cord all the way through.

STEP 5

Turn the cylinder over to show the back. You will have two vertical cords.

STEP 6

Take the right-hand vertical cord and pass it under the left-hand vertical cord so it forms a loop just underneath.

STEP 7

Take the long end of cord and pass it under the left hand loop and up through the middle of the loop.

STEP 8

Turn the cylinder a quarter of a turn towards you and continue to thread the long end of cord under the loop on the top so it comes out of the middle of the loop.

STEP 9

Continue to thread this long end of cord through and under the last loop. This will bring the length of cord back to the start, lying in the opposite direction to the cord secured to the cylinder by the rubber band.

STEP 10

Continue to thread this long length of cord in exactly the same way, following the same pattern you have already created in Steps 6 to 9 so you end up with a double row of cords.

STEP 11

Remove the rubber band and slide the ring off the cylinder. Thread the long end of cord down so it is coming out on the inside of the ring. If using a craft knife, get an adult to help you cut away excess cords and superglue them to the inside of the ring to secure the final shape.

CORD-WRAPPED HAIRBAND

RECYCLE AN OLD HAIRBAND TO GIVE IT A NEW LOOK!

BY TANSY WILSON

MATERIALS
- 8m x 4mm purple paracord
- Hairband
- Small scissors (curved nail scissors)
- Superglue
- Crochet hook (optional)

DIFFICULTY

★★

TOP TIP!

If you have woven the cord really tightly it can be difficult to pull the tail of cord to tighten the loop in Step 10. Try using a crochet hook and hook up the loop a short distance at a time along the hairband, pulling it tightly in sections until you get to the other end.

STEP 1

Take the 8m of 4mm purple para-cord and bind it up loosely so it is easy to hold.

STEP 2

Take one end of the cord and holding it approx. 8cm from one end, lay it along the outside edge of the hairband. When you get to the other end, fold the cord back on itself, leaving a loop overhanging this end approx. 5cm long.

STEP 3

Hold the hairband at the end with the 8cm tail of cord and make sure the long loop that is the length of the hairband from Step 2 is untwisted and laying flat against the hairband (call them centre cords). Take the remaining bound 8m of cord (which we will call the weaving cord) and wrap it around the back of the hairband. Come round to the front, leaving it to rest on top of the centre cords.

STEP 4

Pick up the centre cords and pass the weaving cord around the cords and back behind the hairband.

STEP 5

Lay the centre cords flat on the hairband again and continue the weaving cord round to the front of the hairband to rest on top of the centre cords.

STEP 6

Pick up the centre cords again and wrap the weaving cord around the centre cords and back behind hairband, laying the centre cords back down.

STEP 7

Keep wrapping the weaving cord so it comes back to rest on top of the centre cords. Then it should go around the centre cords and back behind the hairband.

STEP 8

Keep repeating Steps 4 to 7 so the weaving cord wraps around the centre cords and round the hairband one way, then wraps around the centre cords and round the hairband the other way to create the alternating pattern.

STEP 9

When you get to the end of the hairband, pass the end of the cord through the loop.

STEP 10

You can then pull the 8cm tail of cord that you left in Step 2. This will pull the centre cord along the hairband and trap the cord threaded through the loop in Step 9, securing that end. You can then cut away the excess cord, adding a drop of superglue to stop it from fraying.

WHY NOT COVER AN OLD BANGLE? WHY NOT COVER AN OLD BANGLE? WHY N

You will need 5m of cord to cover an adult-sized bangle. It is best to use a larger bangle as the wrapping will make the overall opening size much smaller.

MAKE THIS FABULOUS BELT USING A DECORATIVE BUCKLE. **BY TANSY WILSON**

LADDER RACK BELT

MATERIALS

- 12m x 4mm multicoloured paracord
- 2-part decorative buckle
- Length of 5cm x 2.5cm wood
- Nails and hammer
- Small scissors (curved nail scissors)
- Superglue

DIFFICULTY ★★★

See page 38 for how to make your matching bag handle...

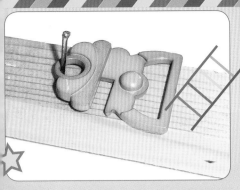

STEP 1

The length of your belt is going to be longer than your braiding board, so for the best results you will need an adult to help you make a simple jig to hold the buckles in place. Measure your waist and then get an adult to cut a length of wood approx. 5cm longer. Hammer a nail close to one end to hold one side of your buckle.

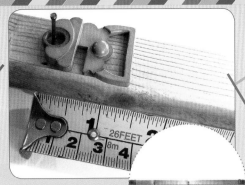

STEP 2

Measure along the wood until you get to your waist measurement including the buckle length. Place the other side of the buckle at this measurement and then hammer another nail in to hold it in place.

STEP 3

Take the 12m length of 4mm multicoloured cord and seal both ends to stop them fraying using a drop of superglue. Fold the cord in half and hold it at the fold, so it becomes a loop. Hold one part of your buckle so the front of the buckle is facing up and thread the loop of cord down through it. Now take both loose ends of the cord and thread them through the loop and pull all the way through so the cord loop is tight against the buckle and facing up.

STEP 4

Hold the other part of the buckle so it also has the front of the buckle facing up. Thread both ends of the cord down through the buckle.

STEP 5

Place your buckles onto the jig so the two cords threaded down in Step 4 become straight and untwisted and are now the correct length for the belt. Hold one end of the cord and thread it down the belt buckle part used in Step 3, making sure it is to the left of the first loop made. Take the other end of cord and thread it down the same belt buckle part, but this time to the right of the loop. Pull all the way through.

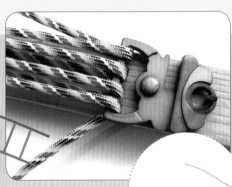

STEP 6

Keeping all the cords untwisted, take the ends of cord and thread them down through the part of the belt buckle used in Step 4. Make sure one is to the left and one is to the right of the threading done in Step 4. This will result in you having six straight, untwisted lengths of cord ready to weave.

STEP 7

It is easiest to hold your wooden jig so the loose cords ready to weave are at the top. Separate them so you have a pair of cords at the left, a pair of cords in the middle and a pair of cords to the right.

STEP 8

Take the far right-hand cord, which is the loose one ready to weave, and thread it under the right pair of cords. Then thread it over the middle pair of cords and then under the left pair of cords. Pull the cord all the way through.

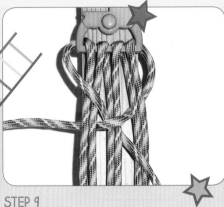

STEP 9

Take the far left-hand cord, which is the loose one ready to weave, and thread it over the left pair of cords. Make sure you are above the cord used in Step 8. Thread it under the middle pair of cords and over the right pair of cords making sure you exit under the cord used in Step 8. Pull the cord all the way through.

STEP 10

Pull both cord ends together so the knot tightens onto the six straight cords between the buckles. Use your fingers to slide the knot up to rest snugly under the buckle.

STEP 11

Repeat Steps 8 to 10 so you start with the far right-hand cord and go under the right pair of cords, over the middle pair of cords and under the left pair of cords. Then take the left-hand cord and starting above the cord just used, go over the left pair of cords, under the middle pair of cords and over the right pair of cords. Pull the cords all the way through so the weave tightens. Slide it up with your fingers.

STEP 12

Keep repeating Step 11 until you reach the other end. Remove the belt from the jig for the final lines of the weave as it will be easier. Finally, ensure you thread the last cords down so the ends that will be cut are at the back of the belt. Cut the ends as close as possible and add a drop of superglue to stop them fraying.

Top tip!

Get an adult to help you make the wooden jig.

Why not?

Make a FUNKY MATCHING STRAP FOR YOUR BAG. YOU WILL NEED 8M OF CORD TO MAKE AN 18CM STRAP. Also add a matching DRAGONFLY BROOCH for that extra special detail (see page 19).

DON'T FORGET TO ADD YOUR DRAGONFLY BROOCH THAT EXTRA SPECIAL DETIAL

BROOCH FROM PAGE 19

38

See page 40 to start making your Cool Clips

COOL CLIPS

TRY THIS SIMPLE TECHNIQUE TO MAKE A WEAVE FOR CLIPS IN A WHOLE VARIETY OF COLOURS. BY TANSY WILSON

MATERIALS

- 1.5m x 4mm red paracord
- 1.5m x 4mm blue paracord
- Carabiner (or any large key ring or alternative clip)
- Small scissors (curved nail scissors)
- Superglue

DIFFICULTY

★ ★

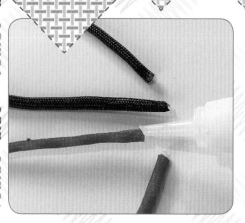

STEP 1

Use 1.5m of each of red and blue 4mm paracord and add superglue to all the ends to stop them from fraying.

STEP 2

Fold the red cord in half and at this halfway point form a 'Z' shape.

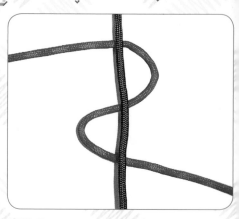

STEP 3

Find the halfway point on the blue cord and at this point, lay the blue cord on top of the red 'Z'.

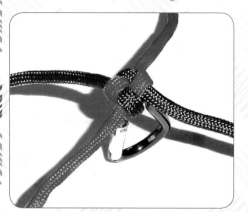

STEP 7

Pick all your cords up and turn the whole thing over so the clip is hanging down. Pull all four cords at the same time. This will tighten them so they form a chequerboard pattern on top of the clip.

STEP 8

Keep each cord coming out of the pattern as straight as possible, like the points on a compass (a red north and south cord, and a blue east and west cord). Take the bottom red cord and fold it over the top, south to north in direction.

STEP 9

Working anticlockwise, take the blue cord on the right and fold it over the top, east to west in direction.

STEP 11

Take the left blue cord and fold it over the left red cord just used in Step 10 and go west to east in direction, threading it under the right red cord. This is threading it through the loop created in Step 8.

STEP 12

Pull all the ends at the same time to tighten the cords and create another layer of chequerboard pattern.

STEP 13

Repeat Steps 8 to 12, but this time go in a clockwise direction so your last cord is now passing east to west and going through the loop created at the start of this layer.